MW01703257

I hope you will find
inspiration and hope ~
peace & blessings ~
♡ Sandra J. Madden

Hearts All Around Us

PRT1114A

Library of Congress Control Number: 2014917878
ISBN-13: 978-1-62086-849-2

Printed in the United States
www.mascotbooks.com

Hearts All Around Us

Sandra A. Madden

Acknowledgments

With deep gratitude, I would like to acknowledge:

- My family, Scott, Alix and Jalen, I love you.
- My late parents, Allesandro and Patricia Smachetti, their spirit is sent to me in many of these hearts.
- Nancy Lubrano, for your gift of the inspiration of hearts and your gift of love and friendship for 40 years, I hold you close to my heart.
- Carolyn Wynn, your love and friendship for 34 years is a blessing, I consider you my sister, and I am grateful to you for your unwavering support of my photography.
- Janet Gallagher, who literally jumped for joy when I told her I was publishing this book—I will always appreciate your caring friendship, giving heart and your support of my artistic endeavor.
- Ryan, Felice, Tracey & Laura, four of the strongest survivors I have been blessed to meet and to have your presence in my life; your perseverance, strength and spirit are to be admired and your kindness and friendship is a treasure to me.
- In support and care of all brain injury survivors, their families and caregivers~your strength, courage and perseverance are to be honored every day.
- Todd Civin, fellow "Orangeman" and friend, if it hadn't been for your kindness and support, I would not have had the courage to follow through on this project.

For all who so generously backed my Kickstarter project to bring my book to fruition, I am thankful for your generosity and your belief in *Hearts All Around Us*, namely:

Alana Warren, Alis Biri, Ann Kerwood, Bettiann Michalik, Dee Citrin, Ed & Lori Tarka, Felice Regan, Greta Ann Madden, Jack & Heidi Babb, Janet Cromer, Janet Gallagher, Jay LaFratta, Jeff, Jill Lindstrom, Joan Tognini, Julie LaPlante, Kellyann Madden, Kevin & Antje, Kimberly Stevens, Kristine Sassorossi, Larry & Leslie Spencer, Laura Mason, LeeAnn Madden, Lehshel Pond, Linda M., Linda & Chuck, Linda Williams, Lynda Herendeen LaVangie, Lynn Riordan, Martha McManus, Mary Gallagher, Maureen, Mindy Newman, Myra Hill, Nancy Guidrey Lovely, Nancy Lubrano, Nicole M. Godaire, Pat Jennings, Paul Smachetti, Penni & Kyle Sadlon, Rhonda Riegel, Rick Penezic, Robert Simpson, Ryan Lynne Farrell, Sally Johnson, Sandy Topalian, Scott Whittier, The Stansky Family, Tina Forster, Todd & Katie, Tom Damoulakis, Wendy Buchanan, Zelinda, and several donors who wish to remain anonymous.

Note from the Author

Several years ago, I attended a screening of a documentary entitled *Shooting Beauty*. This film "chronicles the creation of photographer Courtney Bent's experimental photography program at United Cerebral Palsy (UCP) in Watertown, Massachusetts. For this program, Ms. Bent began adapting cameras and teaching photography to a group of individuals with disabilities at UCP. Her photography workshop was created to provide a new avenue of self-expression through the art of photography for individuals with disabilities, some who had very limited means of communicating." (www.shootingbeauty.org/about)

After seeing this phenomenal film I realized that as a photographer, I have always taken for granted that my hands are able to grasp a camera, that my finger is able to trigger a shutter, and my legs can take me anywhere I want to go to capture the images I have taken since my love of photography began in high school. The world of photography was always open to me and I never realized that an individual with a disABILITY was most likely closed off to this creative world because of mechanics. I was captivated by the images that the photographers from UCP captured and I was educated about their lives; and I was in awe of Courtney Bent and all of her students.

Visit ShootingBeauty.org or go to YouTube.com and search *Shooting Beauty Trailer*, *100 Cameras Project,* and *Cameras Come to Crotched Mountain*. Prepare to be moved, amazed, inspired, and if you are like me, teary-eyed with a full heart.

If you or your loved one are disABLED and unable to take photographs with a traditional camera, or if you feel that you are not a "creative type," please do not let that dissuade you from reading my book and trying photography for the first time or renewing your interest in it. Please don't let a challenge become a roadblock to discovering your inner artist, and discovering that photography is a means to cope with challenges, and find peace and joy.

The following is a short list of websites to research to assist in finding adaptive equipment; additional research can be done online with key search words such as "adaptive camera equipment":

- http://www.abledata.com
- http://www.meetup.com/Valley-Rolling-F-Stops/pages/Wheelchair_Camera_Mounts/
- http://rollingfstop.blogspot.com
- http://conceptusinc.com
- http://www.adaptivetechsolutions.com

"Each of us is an artist, capable of conceiving and creating a vision from the depths of our being." -Dorothy Fadiman

Introduction

It all began with a splotch, a small splotch of yellow mustard.

Nancy, one of my oldest and best friends, emailed me a photograph of a splotch of mustard on a piece of bread, curiously shaped like a heart; she was making a sandwich for her husband's lunch. This little yellow mustard heart and Nancy's thought of finding a heart every day and photographing it intrigued me. Could we find a heart every day?

I began to search every day for what I thought would be an elusive subject, but I have found that for the days I do not discover my "heart of the day," there are days when I find several hearts in so many places and in so many things. As my collection of hearts grew, I realized that this photography project was something more than just a collection of photographs of a simple, universally known shape; the shape that to most signifies love. The heart. To me, this heart signified a means to cope, to find peace and joy, and ultimately, to find the presence of healing in my body, mind, and soul.

For me, the simplicity in the shape of the heart also holds meanings of spirituality. I feel that some of these hearts were sent to me from a higher place, and from loved ones in heaven. It also is a pronouncement of a change in my life, a turning point. It has become entwined with my heart and soul, it has become a tool for coping and healing, for overcoming challenges I have confronted as a brain injury survivor. As someone who, due to traumatic brain injury (TBI), lives with chronic neuropathic pain (burning, stabbing, throbbing, prickling, and numbness in my arms, legs, hands and feet), headaches and "brain chatter" (many brain injury survivors talk about this phenomenon, for me it describes the constant talking and singing I hear in my brain, always in times of quiet but there are times that chatter in my brain fights to be heard over other sounds), cognitive issues, as well as the pain of arthritis.

I discovered something of great significance while hunting for hearts and being behind the camera photographing this beautiful shape, that the focus I needed to find hearts and create my art took the focus away from the noise in my brain ("chatter") and body (pain). *COMPLETELY*.

I am in constant search of a heart in the world around me. It doesn't matter where I am or where I am going, I look everywhere. There are times that I head out on the road with camera in tow just to look for hearts; I believe this searching in itself is beneficial to my brain and aids in the healing process. Although my last neuropsychological test deemed me to have an "average" brain, I still struggle every day with cognitive issues. Since eight years have passed and my pain issues have not been resolved, I feel I will always struggle with neuropathic, arthritic and head pain. After accepting this "new normal" years ago, I can better cope with these issues because of the gifts of photography, and the simple gift of a heart.

Neither Nancy nor I knew that her splotch of mustard, this yellow heart, would become the inspiration to share my photographs and my story. I hope to offer to other brain injury survivors, their caregivers, and anyone who is challenged with a disABILITY or other life challenge, to take up a camera and begin looking for hearts, or something else you can fall in love with, and discover that the simple art of taking photographs may help you cope with the challenges in your life. It may help you find healing powers in discovering the creativity that lives within you, that lives within all of us, and this discovery gives me hope that you will find joy as well.

"Art arises when the secret vision
of the artist and the manifestation
of nature agree to find new shapes."
– Kahlil Gibran

Many in a Pansy

"If instead of a gem, or
even a flower, we should
cast the gift of a loving
thought into the heart
of a friend; that would
be giving as the angels
give."
– George MacDonald

Petite White Flowers

Purple Tinged Petals

White Tulip - Public Gardens

New England Barn

"When you're sad, my Little Star, go out of doors.
It's always better underneath the open sky."

–Eva Ibbotson

Over Hampton Beach

"We shall find peace. We shall hear angels, we shall see the sky sparkling with diamonds."

–Anton Chekhov

Four Perfect Hearts - Sand Dune on Cape Cod

"The golden moments in the stream of life rush past us, and we see nothing but sand; the angels come to visit us, and we only know them when they are gone."

-George Eliot

Toes

The Invisible Injuries

I had always been involved in athletics since middle school, and in my 40s I made a somewhat impetuous decision to buy a new bicycle, a 21-speed Trek. I became so enthralled with, and inspired by, Lance Armstrong. His record-breaking Tour de France wins amazed and inspired me. I was in awe of the feats he accomplished in the cycling world against so many odds (this was prior to his downfall in the cycling world). When I had become serious about bicycling, reaching distances of over forty miles, I knew it was important to wear a helmet, thinking of a cracked skull but not of damage that could potentially happen to my brain. I always wore my helmet, I always felt protected, even when I lost control of my bicycle on a hill and sailed over the handlebars to the asphalt in the summer of 2006. There was no thought to go to the emergency room because I was wearing a helmet and when I got up from the street I could walk, it was only my bicycle that seemed broken. It never occurred to me that I could have suffered a concussion in the accident.

As the day wore on, my shoulder was causing me pain, so I finally decided a visit to the emergency room would be wise. Upon being seen at the emergency room, the doctor asked if I had been wearing a helmet, to which I replied "yes"; there was no mention of the possibility of suffering a concussion and no further discussion was had to alert me to signs of concussion in the days post-accident. I think back to this and realize that even the medical professionals aren't fully educated about TBI. If only the doctor had discussed the potential of concussion and the signs to be aware of, I would have sought help when cognitive issues became, in my mind, problematic.

Immediately after my accident, neuropathic pain became a constant in my life as well as neck pain due to arthritis in my cervical spine, so my primary care physician (PCP) referred me to a neurologist and a spine specialist. In the spring of 2008, my headaches became persistent, and I was living with (and still live with) a constant headache. This chronic pain began to define my life; pain had taken over and with the exception of arthritis, could not be explained.

Many tests were performed to rule out all the diseases in which neuropathic pain was a symptom, and then new symptoms began to emerge—cognitive in nature. When bringing these cognitive issues to the attention of the neurologist, it was attributed to a side effect of the medication I was taking for the neuropathic pain, a medication called Lyrica. I kept telling my neurologist, and even my spine specialist about the cognitive issues at every visit. Time went on and no diagnosis could be made for my neuropathic pain, and the cognitive issues were still being attributed to medicine.

Nearly eighteen months after my bicycle accident, I was visiting the spine specialist for the fourth time. When I got off the elevator to go to my appointment, I found no familiarity in the surroundings. I brought this to the attention of the doctor who quickly replied, "You might have suffered a mild brain injury in your bike accident, let me refer you to a doctor at Spaulding Rehabilitation Hospital."

In January of 2008, I traveled to Spaulding Rehabilitation Hospital in Boston and described the bicycle accident and the cognitive issues I was having and within one half-hour, my new doctor pronounced a diagnosis of Post-Concussive Syndrome. I was flooded with relief and grateful to have a diagnosis for my memory issues.

My "brain injury doctor," as I called him, gave me a script to see a Speech-Language Pathologist (SLP) and on my first visit I was given a brief neuropsychological test. I remember asking the therapist, "Do I really have a brain injury?" to which she answered affirmatively. But, I didn't truly know what having a brain injury meant, I didn't know what questions to ask, and I do not remember her offering any further explanation except to say that recovery from traumatic brain injury is more feasible when the TBI is diagnosed in the first few months; my diagnosis was given eighteen months after my bicycle accident.

In hindsight, I took something positive from my visits with the SLP, and that was to find compensatory strategies to aid in situations where I could not count on my brain. To this day, I still utilize these compensatory strategies every day. At the end of this book, I will list compensatory strategies that I utilize in hopes this information may be of help to some readers.

To complicate matters, in the summer of 2011 I tripped over a garden hose, falling into a cement driveway, striking chin first into the hard surface. Immediately after the fall, all of my pain symptoms increased and the pain levels continued to stay at a higher level; my cognitive issues continued to plague me. My PCP sent me for testing, including an MRI of my neck, and a visit to other specialists, but nothing could be found. I attribute the increased pain and the lingering cognitive issues to a second concussion.

Although my cognitive issues were finally attributed to a diagnosis of Post-Concussive Syndrome, I wouldn't be so fortunate with concern to my neuropathic pain issues and my headaches; to be concise, I would see specialists and undergo years of testing in which a diagnosis eluded me for eight years. In all this time, I was searching on the Internet for any answers I could find for my pain symptoms and only recently stumbled upon a condition called Central Pain Syndrome; so many of the symptoms described "fit me to a T." I printed out all I could find and brought it to my current neurologist. I blurted out to him "This is me!" After "taking everything off the table" (as the neurologist describes it), there is likely a diagnosis of Central Pain Syndrome (CPS); a syndrome caused by brain trauma.

As I reflect on the last eight years, I can remember distinctly the time I asked the first neurologist I had been referred to, "Could the neuropathic pain be caused by my bicycle accident?" He firmly replied "No." I explained again to him that the neuropathic pain started right after the bicycle accident, his answer did not change.

I would be remiss if I did not mention that the Spaulding Rehabilitation doctor that diagnosed my Post-Concussive Syndrome and was aware of my undiagnosed neuropathic pain suggested that my brain could be interpreting non-painful signals as painful; that the signals were reflecting pain. At that time, I could not accept his explanation because it would mean that it could never be fixed and the pain would be permanent. However, there was no mention of a syndrome called Central Pain Syndrome. Had the CPS been presented to me, I would have stopped searching then and there for a reason for my chronic pain. The complication of having arthritis in my cervical spine led to my advocating to my PCP and other doctors for multiple MRIs of my neck, convinced that there was impingement on nerves causing the neuropathic pain. Many years would pass and although there was degeneration, there was no nerve impingement to be found.

It has been a long eight years searching for answers, I cannot dwell on the possibility that the answer may have been there many years ago.

Tipped Tombstone

"He spake well who said that graves are the footprints of angels."

-Henry Wadsworth Longfellow

In the Moss

Collage on a Tombstone

In Memory of Taylor

"Make yourself familiar with the angels, and behold them frequently in spirit; for, without being seen, they are present with you."

-St. Francis of Sales

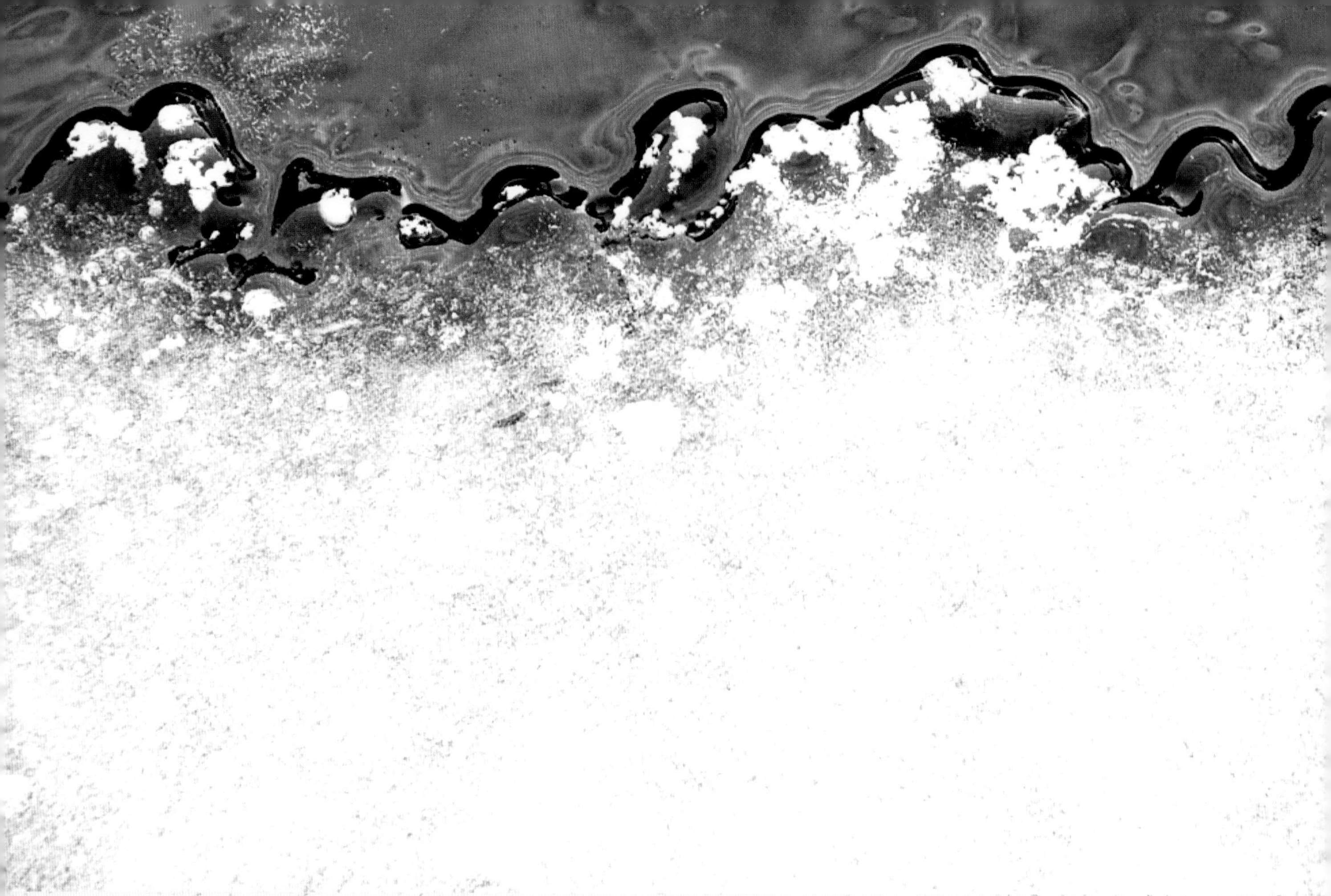

Abstract Heart in Ice

"Ever felt an angel's breath in the gentle breeze? A teardrop in the falling rain? Hear a whisper amongst the rustle of leaves? Or been kissed by a lonely snowflake? Nature is an angel's favorite hiding place."

–Terri Guillemets

Ice over Christmas Lights

Ice Sculpture

Leaves like a Puzzle

New Hampshire Woods

"Life is made up, not of great sacrifices or duties,
but of little things, in which smiles and kindness,
and small obligations given habitually, are what
preserve the heart and secure comfort."

-Humphry Davy

"Write it on your heart that every day is the best day in the year."

-Ralph Waldo Emerson

Stock # 11242, 11193 6 Available
NISSAN

"Whatever we are waiting for – peace of mind, contentment, grace, the inner awareness of simple abundance – it will surely come to us, but only when we are ready to receive it with an open and grateful heart."
–Sarah Ban Breathnach

Hosta Leaf

"The best and most beautiful things in the world cannot be seen or even touched – they must be felt with the heart."

-Helen Keller

Perched Butterfly

Wings like a Heart

"With stillness comes the benediction of peace."

-Eckhart Tolle

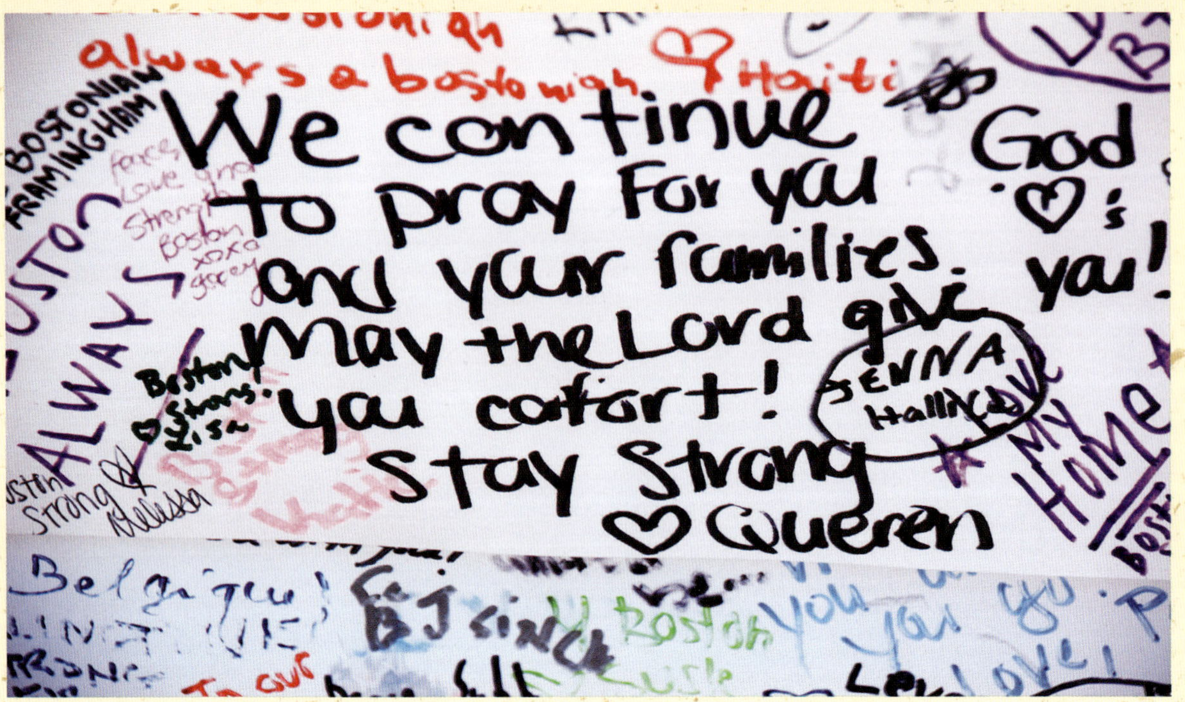

"The world breaks everyone, and afterward, some are strong at the broken places."

-Ernest Hemingway

Heartbreak Hill - 2014 Boston Marathon

"What lies behind you and what lies in front of you, pales in comparison to what lies inside of you."

- Ralph Waldo Emerson

"The greatest test of courage on earth is to bear defeat without losing heart." – *Robert Green Ingersoll*

In memory and in honor of all affected by the 2013 Boston Marathon bombings, may love and peace bless your hearts.

Tiny Pancake Heart on Spatula

Strawberry

Juicy Tomato

Hot Cocoa

"Even as the stone of the fruit must break, that its heart may stand in the sun, so must you know pain…accept the seasons of your heart, even as you have always accepted the seasons that pass over your fields…"

-Khalil Gibran

Cut from Loaf of Bread

Unexpected Blessings

As I reviewed my photographs for consideration for publication, the proverbial "light bulb" went off. Hearts bring me a reminder of the unexpected blessings of sustaining a traumatic brain injury. My late mother used to say frequently, "Everything happens for a reason," and while there are times that this sentiment won't make the bad things better, it puts the bad things into perspective in my mind and heart, and helps me to endure and find appreciation for what is good. Approval for social security disability presented me a gift of time to volunteer, to think about helping others, and focus my mind on something other than cognitive deficits and pain. In addition to several organizations such as The Red Cross Food Pantry and the Alzheimer's Association, I found that the Brain Injury Association of Massachusetts was in need of volunteers and I did not hesitate to offer my time. During a three-year period, I was given projects that would draw on my strengths from previous work experience and interests, and volunteered longer hours, which would give me the confidence to feel I could return to the workforce. In 2012, I was offered a full-time position as Administrative Assistant at the Brain Injury Association of Massachusetts. Working in an environment of understanding and acceptance of my cognitive issues and knowing that each day, my support of colleagues at work is helping BIA-MA to support brain injury survivors, caregivers, and family members is a blessing beyond measure.

We can never anticipate at the dawn of each day the blessings that await us, the moment when we meet someone new and have hopes that this special person will always be part of our life. Twenty-nine years have passed, and my late mother's wisdom still whispers in my mind. If not for my brain injury, there are some very special friends and colleagues I would not have had the opportunity to meet and build important relationships with. Blessings abound and I am grateful!

"Some people come into our lives and quickly go. Some stay for a while, leave footprints on our hearts, and we are never, ever the same."

–Flavia Weedn

Duo

"It is not so much for its
beauty that the forest makes
a claim upon men's hearts,
as for that subtle something,
that quality of air, that
emanation from old trees,
that so wonderfully changes
and renews a weary spirit."
-Robert Louis Stevenson

Dudley Pond - Douglas

Fat

Best Friend's Art is a Gift

"A friend may well be reckoned the masterpiece of nature."
-Ralph Waldo Emerson

A Flurry of Clovers in my Backyard

Rock Ledge in Woods of New Hampshire

"Keep close to Nature's heart...and break clear away, once in a while, and climb a mountain or spend a week in the woods. Wash your spirit clean."

-John Muir

Fire Hydrant

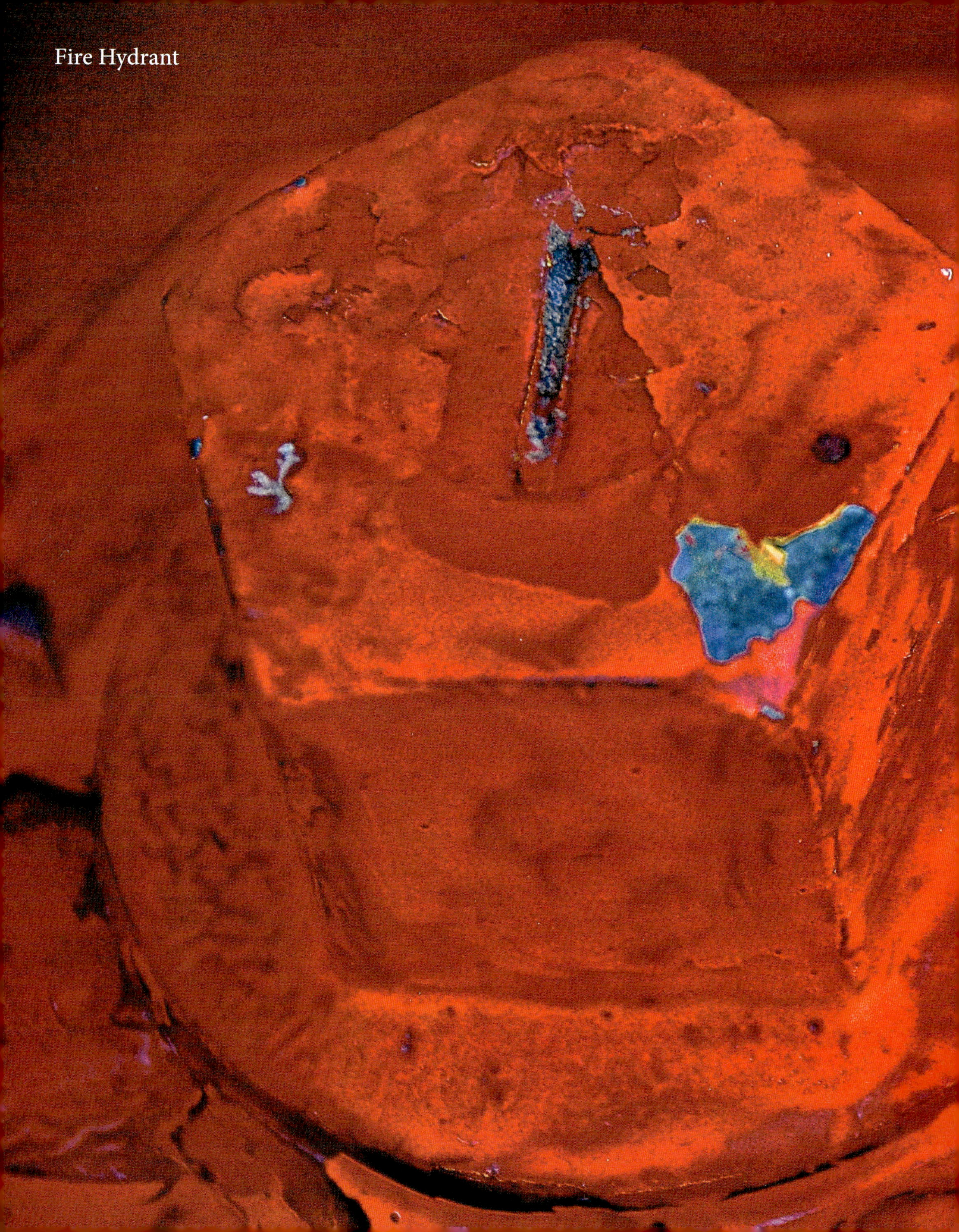

"The unthankful heart...discovers no mercies; but let the thankful heart sweep through the day and, as the magnet finds the iron, so it will find, in every hour, some heavenly blessings!"

-Henry Ward Beecher

“We all should know that diversity makes for a rich tapestry, and we must understand that all the threads of the tapestry are equal in value no matter what their color.”

–Maya Angelou

"All I ever wanted was to reach out and touch another human being not just with my hands but with my heart."

-Tahereh Mafi

George at Jamaica Pond

"It is time for parents to teach young people early on that in diversity there is beauty and there is strength."

-Maya Angelou

Perfect/Abstract

In photograph after photograph, I am continually astonished by the perfect and the abstract heart shapes found in the woods, on the beach, in the forest, in flowers, on concrete, steel and glass, in the grass and in the sky. At times, it might require some imagination to find that beautiful shape, but my photographer's eye and mind sees hearts everywhere.

How do you explain a strand of seaweed, shaped perfectly like a heart upon the wet sand, or the multiple hearts that appear in the sand dunes, or the heart in the bark of a very old tree? This is when I feel a spiritual connection at work.

The shape of the heart is healing for many reasons. The shape itself signifies love, and love is a healing gift. There are times I feel the heart has been sent to me to find; it is a message or gift from my parents in heaven. It is exciting when I find a heart in nature, like a treasure hunt, with continuous amazement that this shape is found in, on, and around inanimate objects in my world, not drawn by human hands.

I am joyful and amazed at times, upon discovering every new heart awaiting me, awaiting my camera to capture the beautiful shape.

Please know that the hearts in these photographs appeared to me exactly as you see them, I did not "Photoshop" any images to create a heart shape; I did not create any of these hearts with my hands.

Photography focuses my mind and my thoughts, stops the brain chatter, and removes all focus from my pain. It allows me to be mindful because I am focused so intently on the objects I am photographing and their surroundings, it is my meditation when I have failed time and time again trying traditional meditation. With traditional meditation, the voices and sounds in my brain interferes, the noise of my pain interferes, and I become frustrated; this is not the result I should be achieving through meditation. However, when I take my camera and head out on a search for hearts, I am at peace.

I read in a tweet from Everyday Mindfulness (@mindfuleveryday) that "When you focus on something else, anxiety lessens, because your brain can't be in two places at once."

Start looking for hearts. You will be surprised where you find them, and if you keep looking, you will be blessed with more and more hearts. The feeling I get when I find a heart, is hard to explain, but it has the capacity to make me very happy.

Remember, you can use your cellphone camera, a simple "point and shoot" camera, or a high-end digital SLR. It doesn't matter what kind of camera, it doesn't matter if you get a great photo or not, it is the joy you can find in creating art, joy that will help you cope, heal, and find peace. Yes, every photograph is art created by you, so create it often!

Escape to a quiet place and take photographs, listen to the quiet, listen to the bugs and the birds and the wind, look up to the sky and look around and down. Or go to the beach, listen to the beautiful sound of the waves crashing, walk up and down the beach in search of your hearts and find peace in this environment. Be mindful of your place in the space you are in. Find your subject and lose yourself in your photography, your art. May you find the healing and joy that I have found these last few years, which has bestowed on me the gift of acceptance of my "new normal" and the ability to find the blessings of a changed life.

"A laugh, to be joyous, must flow from a joyous heart, for without kindness, there can be no true joy."

-Thomas Carlyle

Happy Birthday!

Antique Ford

*"The less you open your heart to others,
the more your heart suffers."*
-Deepak Chopra

Door Lock - Boston Waterfront

Rusty Bridge

Joined Hearts

Blue

Stone Wall of Abandoned Factory

"Man never made any material as resilient as the human spirit."

-Bern Williams

"If you are seeking creative ideas, go out walking. Angels whisper to a man when he goes for a walk."

-Raymond Inman

"Those who contemplate the beauty of the earth find reserves of strength that will endure as long as life lasts. There is something infinitely healing in the repeated refrains of nature – the assurance that dawn comes after night, and spring after winter."

-Rachel Carson

"Everything is blooming most recklessly; if it were voices instead of colors, there would be an unbelievable shrieking into the heart of the night."
-Rainer Maria Rilke

"Nature never did betray the heart
that loved her."
-William Wordsworth

Old Vines

Leaf Among the Flowers

"Spread love everywhere you go: first of all in your own home. Give love to your children, to your wife or husband, to a next door neighbor...let no one ever come to you without leaving better and happier. Be the living expression of God's kindness; kindness in your face, kindness in your eyes, kindness in your smile, kindness in your warm greeting."

–Mother Teresa

Peeling Bark

"I'm such a fan of nature, and being with the trees every day fills me with joy."

-Scott Blum

Near Rhode Island

"In all things of nature, there is something of the marvelous."

–Aristotle

Blackstone Valley Sign

Bicycle Sign on Cape Cod

"Don't look for big things, just do small things with great love…the smaller the thing, the greater must be our love."
-Mother Teresa

Three Hearts on Bridge

Colorful Hearts on Cape Cod Beach

This is Seaweed!

My Brain, My Body, My Syndromes

Have you ever heard of Post-Concussive Syndrome? *Post-Concussive Syndrome is a collection of symptoms that some people develop after they have had concussion.* It is a complication of concussion. Symptoms of Post-Concussive Syndrome can include headache, dizziness, and memory and concentration problems (www.patient.co.uk/health/post-concussion-syndrome).

A concussion is a mild traumatic brain injury (TBI). *A traumatic brain injury is an injury to the head caused by an external physical force.* Most traumatic brain injuries are caused by accidents or assaults to the skull that are sufficiently hard to cause the brain to move within the skull or to cause the skull to break and directly injure the brain. (www.biama.org)

Awareness surrounding traumatic brain injury is on the rise, yet, there is a long way to go among professionals, young and old athletes, and parents. The word "concussion" was not in any vocabulary I had known; my fifteen-year-old son has played hockey since he was five years old, and has never suffered a concussion. I played sports in high school, and women's rugby in college, and never suffered a concussion. I don't recall hearing in the past the symptoms that are attributed to a concussion. Certainly, I did not know that a concussion is a traumatic brain injury (TBI). Sometimes, there is no literature handed to you when you or your children engage in playing a sport, warning you of concussions and their symptoms, and in some sports we play, the inherent danger of multiple concussions.

♥

As defined by the National Institute of Neurological Disorders and Stroke (NINDS), "Central Pain Syndrome is a neurological condition caused by damage to or dysfunction of the central nervous system (CNS), which includes the brain, brainstem, and spinal cord. This syndrome can be caused by spinal cord or ***brain trauma***, Parkinson's disease, stroke, multiple sclerosis, tumors, or epilepsy. The character of the pain associated with this syndrome differs widely among individuals partly because of the variety of potential causes. Central Pain Syndrome may affect a large portion of the body or may be more restricted to specific areas, such as hands or feet. The extent of pain is usually related to the cause of the CNS injury or damage. Pain is typically constant, may be moderate to severe in intensity, and is often made worse by touch, movement, emotions, and temperature changes, usually cold temperatures. Individuals experience one or more types of pain sensations, the most prominent being burning. Mingled with the burning may be sensations of "pins and needles;" pressing, lacerating, or aching pain; and brief, intolerable bursts of sharp pain similar to the pain caused by a dental probe on an exposed nerve. Individuals may have numbness in the areas affected by the pain. The burning and loss of touch sensations are usually most severe on the distant parts of the body, such as the feet or hands. Central Pain Syndrome often begins shortly after the causative injury or damage, but may be delayed by months or even years, especially if it is related to post-stroke pain."

The eight-year journey to a diagnosis is the reason I am including this lengthy definition of Central Pain Syndrome, it is significant, as I believe there may be other brain injury survivors who have been dealing with chronic pain for a long time and for which there has been no diagnosis or explanation.

♥

I have created a blog in anticipation that readers will interact with me after reading *Hearts All Around Us*. My hope is that we will become a community, with one helping another, having a platform to share our thoughts and photographs. The blog can be found at www.heartsallaroundus.blogspot.com. Help me make this new blog a success—please send photographs of the hearts that you find and indicate where the photograph was taken, does it have any special meaning, does taking photographs provide a means to cope with your challenges, has taking photographs provided healing? Photographs and comments can be emailed to me for posting to the blog at: photogofhearts@gmail.com

My Compensatory Strategies for Short-Term Memory Issues:

- Place your keys and purse, backpack, or briefcase in the same location in your home every time you come home, and when you go out, your keys and purse, backpack, or briefcase will always be in the same place.
- When parking at stores, many stores have words on the exterior, such as at Target; park down the aisle from the word on the building every time you go to that store. Or park in the farthest lane to the right or left of the store, you may have to walk a little extra but you will always be able to remember where you parked.
- Keep a notebook and pen with you in your vehicle, or in your purse, backpack, or briefcase.
- If you have a Smartphone, utilize the tools (such as alarms to remind you to take medication and a calendar to track appointments with alerts to remind you of the upcoming appointments) and research online the various "apps" available, many are free.

- Write a "To Do" list every day.
- Create bookmarks on your computer for websites you visit frequently.
- Write down "sign-ins" and passwords for websites you visit and keep them near your computer.
- Send yourself an email message or leave yourself a voicemail message if you need a reminder for something and are unable to write it down.
- If you do not want to forget to bring something to work or school the next day, place it with your purse, backpack, or briefcase the night before; alternately, place a sticky note or tape a note to your front door above the doorknob reminding you "Do not forget ___________________".

If you or a loved one has suffered a brain injury, reach out to your local Brain Injury Association or Brain Injury Alliance for information and resources and to inquire about support groups in your area; you can search for these organizations on the Internet for their websites and their social media presence (Facebook, Twitter, Pinterest, and Instagram). If you are not sure where to turn, contact the Brain Injury Association of America at 800-444-6443 or visit http://www.biausa.org

"Walk tall as the trees, live strong as the mountains, be gentle as the spring winds, keep the warmth of the summer sun in your heart and the great spirit will always be with you."

–Native American Proverb

"I am grateful for the magic, mystery and majesty of nature – my loyal friend and companion – always there, welcoming and waiting for me to come; to be healed."
–Tom North